67 REASONS WHY CATS ARE BETTER THAN DOGS

by

Jack Shepherd

NATIONAL GEOGRAPHIC

Washington, D.C.

For Princess Cuteyface.
You are lazy and greedy, but I like you.

CONTENTS

Introduction

Anyone who's not completely delusional already knows that cats are superior to dogs in every way, from their delicate noses to their impressive "purr" feature, to their ability to perform advanced calculus when you're not looking (and when they're in the mood, which is never). But ever since the first time some hunter-gatherer took a mangy wolf-hound onto his hearth and found that he was able to tolerate the fleas and the dog breath and the complete *inability* to do advanced calculus, there has been a truly unfortunate misconception that dogs are perfect, and that cats are, like, "too aloof" or whatever.

Well! This book clears that up using *science*. If you are not fully convinced that cats are better than dogs after reading these devastatingly powerful, and not totally made up, arguments for the clear superiority of individuals of the feline persuasion, well then, you should probably get a dog instead. It's fine; just don't expect any sympathy when there's no one around to help you with your calculus homework.

Chapter ONE

ATHLETICISM

While your neighbor's dog is in the yard chasing her own tail as if doing so is an Olympic event, your cat sits quietly at the window, watching, taking it all in, and keeping her own counsel. This is because she is taking notes. She's analyzing every errant move in order to hone her body into that of a perfect athlete through the sheer force of her mind. And if you ever gave her the chance *and* she happened to feel like it at the moment (which she wouldn't), she could excel at any feat of athleticism she set her mind to.

REASON #1

Cats are better at pickup basketball.

It is a common occurrence in "pickup" or "street" basketball for cats to "take it to the hole" and then swagger off the court, leaving their opponents shocked and frightened.

Sadly, for dogs, "pickup basketball"
refers to a more limited set of skills.

Natural ballers, a cat's vertical jump can be up to five times as high as its height. By comparison, LeBron James can only vertically jump around *half* his height, which is one of the many reasons cats are uninterested in professional basketball.

REASON #2

Cats make for a more reliable sled team.

These cats,
with only a stuffed reindeer
to help them, have pulled their
beloved owners over
700 miles in a race across
the bitter snows of Alaska.

Shamefully, this dog has given up
midway through the race, compelling
his team to push *him* the rest of the way
through the snow.

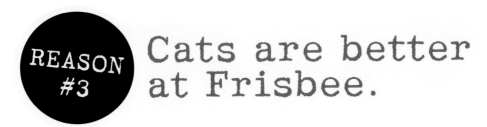

REASON #3

Cats are better at Frisbee.

This picture depicts a dog dropping an easy goal in ultimate Frisbee—a sadly common occurrence.

This image captures the moment
immediately after a cat has executed
an impressive reverse steal
by employing the wedge defense.

REASON #4

Dogs are awful ballroom dancers.

Cats, in fairness, lack enthusiasm, but on the rare and exquisite occasions when they can be persuaded to dance, the sheer beauty of their craft can bring an audience to tears.

Ballroom dancing requires enthusiasm, grace, dexterity, stamina, and *style*. Dogs only possess enthusiasm.

REASON #5

Cats have a higher vertical leap.

The feline high jump is an incredibly competitive event, and world records are broken every time someone finds a higher place to store the dry food.

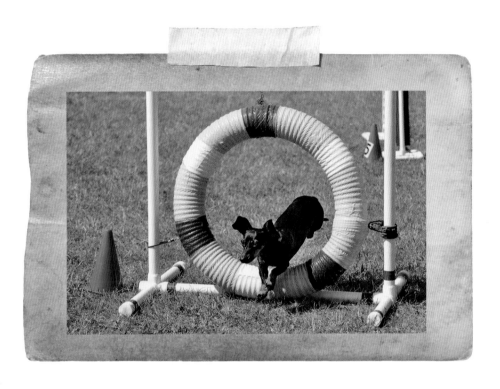

No one has ever bothered to record
the results of the canine competition.

REASON #6

Cats are masters of yoga.

Between achieving feats of athleticism, cats keep loose, limber, and mentally centered by maintaining extremely complicated yoga positions.

Most dogs don't make it past
the beginner class.

REASON #7 Cats are better surfers.

There is no denying that dogs have *some* surfing skill. Here, for instance, a dog surfs an unimpressive wave with the help of a human surf instructor.

In this picture, a cat who has spent the entire day surfing impressive waves at a surf competition now surfs the Web to check weather conditions for tomorrow's grueling day on the board.

Cats are better midfielders.

This dog, attempting to understand the offside rule in soccer, has merely succeeded in chewing on the ball.

This cat,
meanwhile,
has transcended
soccer entirely.
This cat *is* soccer.

REASON #9

Cats are better at table tennis.

A cat poses for a victory shot
after dispatching a series
of opponents with her devastating
forepaw pendulum serve.

Here, a dog cheats at table tennis.

REASON #10

Cats are faster.

Here, a cat easily outruns
a fox without even really
looking where she's going.

Whereas in this photo,
a dog that has been easily
caught by a baby fox doesn't
even try to run, but merely
looks glum and defeated.

Chapter TWO

INTELLECT

Nobody likes a know-it-all, but having someone in the family who projects a sense of intellectual superiority is essential to the smooth running of any household. And you're not going to get that from old Fido sitting in the corner trying to figure out how to lick himself without dropping his toy.

Cats, however, can be relied upon to keep you humble and grounded with their helpful combination of aloofness and contempt. In a way that makes you a *better person*, cats can imply with just a glance that they know more than you ever will. This is because they do.

REASON #11

Cats are better at chess.

This photograph shows a cat memorizing Capablanca's greatest chess endings by playing them through and through against herself.

Meanwhile, this dog is (hilariously) attempting to use the Sicilian defense against a queen's pawn opening. A five-year-old could see through such a poor strategy.

REASON #12

Cats know how to follow directions.

As these telling pictures show . . .

dogs and cats have a very different
relationship with understanding
basic instructions.

REASON #13

Cats are more engaging conversationalists.

This candid photograph shows a cat expertly holding forth on the political news of the day with her human companion.

Having run out of conversation topics, these dogs are getting drunk at 10:30 in the morning.

[CAT FACT] Siamese cats are world-renowned for being excellent communicators. The chattiest breed of cat, they can learn dozens of different meows and like to keep their people informed about their daily activities.

Cats are intellectually honest.

In this photo, an unfortunate canine attempts to squeeze himself through the cat door. He will not succeed because he is not being intellectually honest with himself.

Here, one of the great cat minds of this generation tackles the "feather duster conundrum" (previously thought to be insoluble) with integrity, tenacity, and the sheer power of positive thinking.

Cats are better students.

The worst thing about this photo is not the dishonesty of a dog who has just obtained a fake online diploma for a small fee, but rather the look of genuine pride on the smug animal's face.

Such rampant abuse of academic ethics becomes even more distressing when you consider the countless cats, like this one, struggling to break the fur ceiling and obtain an advanced degree despite a clear institutional bias against feline students in universities.

REASON #16 **Cats are better problem solvers.**

Cats commonly use their lateral thinking skills to solve massively complex logic puzzles, such as the classic "inaccessible-toy-mouse-beyond-the-door" brainteaser pictured here.

Dogs, however, find the very concept of "door"
to be intellectually out of reach.

Cats are better engineers.

This unfortunate family went for
the cheaper "canine engineer" option
and will likely be watching reruns forever.

Whereas in this photo, an expert* feline engineer takes a well-deserved rest after achieving the impossible and hooking up his owners' HDMI output to their home theater receiver.

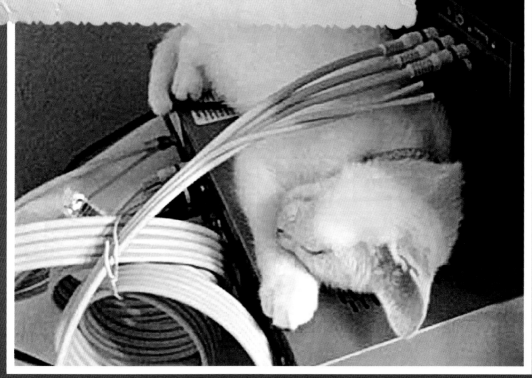

[CAT FACT]

*Actually, studies designed to test a cat's grasp of cause and effect have shown that a cat's understanding of physics and engineering is elementary at best. But who really pays attention to "studies"?

Chapter THREE

COMPANIONSHIP

If slavish devotion is what you crave, you can find a lovely mutt at your local shelter, and good luck. But think about the real relationships in your life, the connections to others that have informed and improved you. You'll find, upon reflection, that any true connection between two souls—any real instance of that intangible thing we call "love"—tends to consist of roughly **10** percent devotion and **90** percent frustration and betrayal.

The point is—cats will give you companionship that is actually meaningful. So what if they break your heart every now and then? That's how love is supposed to feel.

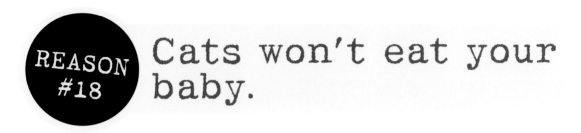

REASON #18

Cats won't eat your baby.

Dogs, when left alone with a baby for even a second, begin to think that it must be snack time.

Cats, on the other hand, make excellent and
responsible babysitters. Some babies nurtured
by cats even learn to play new instruments,
and in a few cases, to speak foreign languages.

REASON #19

Cats are always there for you.

Cats want to be with you, no matter where you are. Regardless of the time, the place, or the convenience, your feline friend will always be there for you.

Dogs, on the other hand, will take any opportunity
they can to pack their stuff and leave
in the middle of the night.

Cats will love you for as long as you live.

Cats will age gracefully with you; they will learn, change, and grow as you learn, change, and grow. Like this beautiful cat with his very best friend in the world, they will comfort and support you throughout the entirety of your life.

Here, a heartless dog informs his owner
that he is leaving her for a younger woman.

 CAT FACT

Your cat literally slows down her aging process to be with you.
During their first two years of life, kittens age rapidly, living
the equivalent of 24 human years. After two years, each cat year
equals about four human years.

REASON #21

Cats worry about you while you are away.

Dogs watch at the window to ensure that you have gone, then proceed to snoop through your medicine cabinet.

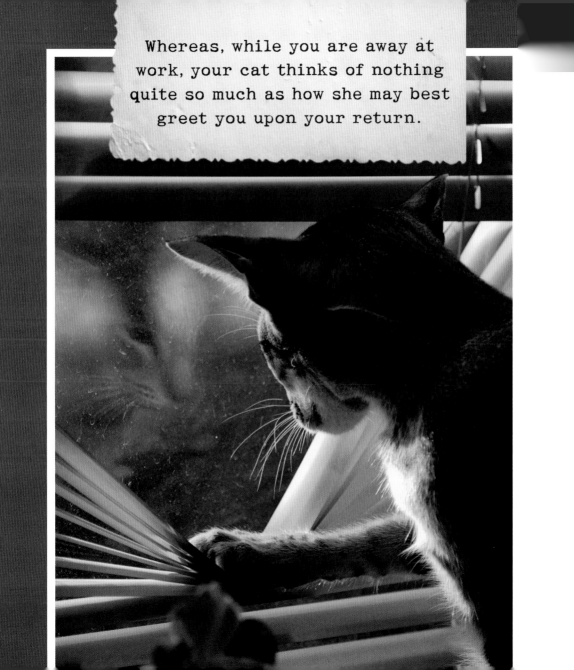

Whereas, while you are away at work, your cat thinks of nothing quite so much as how she may best greet you upon your return.

REASON #22 Cats always remember your birthday.

Dogs will make a point of getting up early on your birthday and eating all your cake.

Cats are extremely careful to make sure that they never have plans on your birthday (or any of the days leading up to it, just to be safe).

Happy Birthday Dennis

REASON #23

Cats will protect your family.

Here, a vigilant guard cat stands watch over the nursery throughout the night.

This paranoid dog is scared of the monster under the bed and has selfishly engaged the services of a guard baby to protect him.

REASON #24

A cat will be there for you when you've had a rough day.

Observe this cat, listening attentively
and with empathy, as his friend
pours out his heart about
a difficult day.

The best you can hope for from a dog
is that he will tell you to Google a psychiatrist
and then promptly fall asleep.

The ability to rotate their ears 180° independently from each other gives cats phenomenal hearing abilities. This makes them excellent listeners, and the irony that most of us choose to fill those refined ears with nonsense and baby talk is not lost on them.

REASON #25

Cats never overstay their welcome.

When a cat guest comes to stay, not only will he keep his visit short and sweet, but he also will thank you for your hospitality by helping with the chores.

It is inadvisable to invite a dog guest to stay. The very first words that any young dog learns are, "Hey man, is it cool if I crash on your couch for a few weeks?"

Chapter FOUR

CHARITY

It is often said of cats that they are not always kind, but this is because they do not boast of their good deeds. For a cat, true philanthropy is in the grateful smile of a child, the dawning understanding of a young student, the joyful glow of a person who has been suddenly enriched.

   To put it more plainly, cats are the very backbone of our society. In fact, any time cats disappear for a day or so and then suddenly reappear as if nothing has happened, it is because they have been out helping the indigent and the needy. And yes, sure, sleeping in the bushes. Even a cat needs to take a break sometimes. Why are we even talking about this? Have you ever seen a dog volunteering at a soup kitchen? No. OK, then.

REASON #26

Cats help the helpless.

Here, a cat prepares to give her last
dollar to a blind orphan
in need of a kidney transplant.

This dog has just stolen money
from the same orphanage. Blind little Jimmy will
just have to make do with his old, broken kidneys.

REASON #27

Cats take time to volunteer.

This touching photograph shows a cat who has taken time out of his busy day to chop vegetables at a soup kitchen.

Meanwhile, over in Fancytown,
fat-cat dogs wait impatiently
to be served four-course meals
by their butlers.

REASON #28

Cats comfort the afflicted.

In this moving photograph,
a cat takes time out of her busy day
to help an injured dog test the durability
of his face cone.

Dogs, on the other hand, see any occasion when they are around sick people as an opportunity to soak up all the attention for themselves.

CAT FACT

Cats have magical healing powers. More specifically, scientists believe that both cats and their people can gain health benefits from purring—the frequency of a purr, around 25 hertz, promotes wound and bone healing and relieves pain.

REASON #29

Cats always lend a helping hand.

Look at this cat patiently teaching a human how to use a water fountain.

Meanwhile, a dog in the same park
maliciously pranks an innocent young girl
by spraying water on her as she walks past.

REASON #30

Cats organize charity drives.

KISSING BOOTH

Most cats spend their spare time organizing charity drives, such as this clever use of a kissing booth to raise money for animal shelters.

In fairness, dogs also sometimes organize
charity drives, but theirs never make any money.

REASON #31

Cats are pillars of the spiritual community.

Instead of squandering his Sunday sleeping in, this selfless animal has volunteered as a pew-warmer at his local church.

These dogs are late for services because
they were watching the football game.

REASON #32

Cats are incredibly civic-minded.

Here, this Good Samaritan collects money to build his local preschool a playground.

In this horrifying photo, a dog stands guard over
the very same playground to ensure that no child
will ever frolic there.

The heartbeat of a cat is about twice as fast as that of a human.
This is almost certainly because cats have two times as much love.

Chapter FIVE

ARTISTRY

When cats set their mind to creating a piece of art, they can work in any style and with any medium. But tragically, they rarely bother to set their mind to such things because they are philosophers first, and artists second. They've sacrificed the easel for the armchair, and the loss to the arts is incalculable. Dogs, meanwhile, eat their own poop.

With an artistic eye comes an artistic temperament, and this is also why one often finds cats gazing contemplatively into the middle distance. This is usually because they are considering the infinite, and you should leave them to their contemplation. In other instances, they are considering vomiting up a hair ball, and you should gently move them away from the rug.

Cats have amazing fashion sense.

There is a reason why **40 percent of** working models in the fashion industry right now are feline —it's because most young people aspire to be like them, and the design houses know it. Why? Because cats look fantastic when they dress up.

Dogs, however, are imitators, not innovators. And it shows.

REASON #34

Cats are musically gifted.

Here, a brilliant feline musician plays avant-garde composer John Cage's classic piece "4'33"" for stunned onlookers.

Despite countless hours of piano lessons,
when asked to play something,
this dog just sits at the piano in silence
for four and a half minutes and then leaves.

REASON #35

Cats make beautiful headwear.

Whether it's for Halloween, Thanksgiving, or just for the sheer joy of it, cats are known for the artistry and skill they bring to the task of knitting festive headwear to brighten any gathering.

Dogs? Less so.

REASON #36

Cats have artistic vision.

This cat is overseeing the painting and decoration of a house, employing an acute sensibility for color, shape, and overall vision.

This dog is stuck on a ladder.

 CAT FACT

Cats have been art stars for millennia—they can be found posing prettily in ancient Egyptian paintings and carvings from 4,000 years ago.

REASON #37

Cats are trendsetters.

Ever at the forefront of fashion, cats are as commonly found in the avant-garde houses of style as they are seen in the pages of mainstream magazines.

If you ever have the singular misfortune
to find yourself at an experimental
dog fashion show, you will regret it for
the rest of your life.

REASON
#38

Cats have a refined
sensibility.

These cats
are
contemplating
the subtle use
of color
and
contrast
in a
watercolor
by one of
their
feline friends.

This bored animal is wondering if there are any doggy treats in the gallery's gift shop.

The expression that beauty is in the eye of the beholder could well have been written about a cat: The eye color of a cat can range from lavender to blue to orange to brown. All kittens are born with blue eyes; they change into their permanent color around three months.

REASON #39

Cats make the best self-portraits.

Cats aren't usually vain enough to make self-portraits, but when pressed to do so, the results are always tasteful, intricate, and inspired.

Dog self-portraits tend to consist of exactly the sort of over-the-top, self-obsessed showboating that you would expect.

Cats have an artistic temperament.

With a combination of intellect and attunement to nature, most cats are also inherently artistic. Although they rarely write down their creations, you can always tell, either from posture or facial expression, when a cat is about to compose a beautiful poem.

Dogs also send clear signals when they are composing poetry. When you detect these signals, it is extremely important that you head quickly but calmly for the nearest exit—a dog's attempts at verse can easily make one physically ill.

Chapter SIX

COURAGE

As we know from Socrates, courage is a form of knowledge. Courage is knowledge about when to hold fast and face your fears and when to hide under the bed because guests are over. Courage is knowledge about when to stand up to your adversaries and when to run up a tree and get stuck up there until the fire department comes. Courage is knowledge about when to be brave and do the difficult, but necessary, thing and when to meow piteously because the vet is trying to take your temperature. Courage, in short, is built into the very DNA of the common house cat.

REASON #41

Cats face their adversaries head-on.

It is an old and wise adage that "Even the most fearsome footwear is no match for a determined cat."

This dog
is frightened
by socks.

[CAT FACT] Despite a lack of opposable thumbs, some (highly evolved) cats are actually able to manipulate their toes independently—much like a fluffier version of a velociraptor from *Jurassic Park*.

REASON #42

Cats are not afraid of bears.

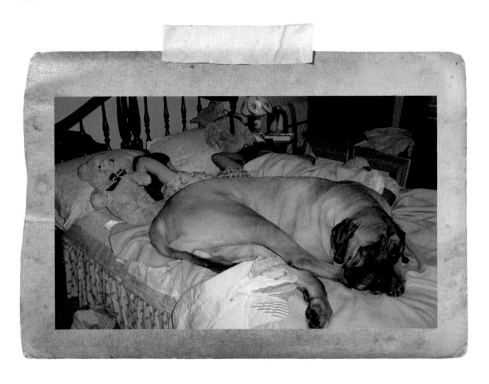

This miserable dog is unable to sleep
because he lives in perpetual fear of the bears
watching him from the pillows.

Whereas, the reason you so rarely
see bears around house cats is simply
because bears are terrified of house cats.
In this rare example of such a meeting,
a frightened bear tries to slink
out of danger as quietly
and quickly as possible.

REASON #43

Cats are not afraid to own up to their mistakes.

Despite abundant evidence to the contrary,
this craven dog is attempting
to look his owner in the eye
and say that he "found it this way."

With the courage of a lion, this admirable c
willing to face the consequences of her unfo
but completely understandable mistak

I PEED
ON THE
HAMSTER

REASON #44

Cats face their fears through daily affirmation.

Cats spend the first part of the morning metaphorically confronting their own demons. This is why they are so often tired throughout the rest of the day.

Dogs are just vain. And they don't
understand metaphors.

Dogs are paranoid conspiracy theorists.

This cat is wearing a tasteful aluminum headpiece simply because it happens to be the latest fashion.

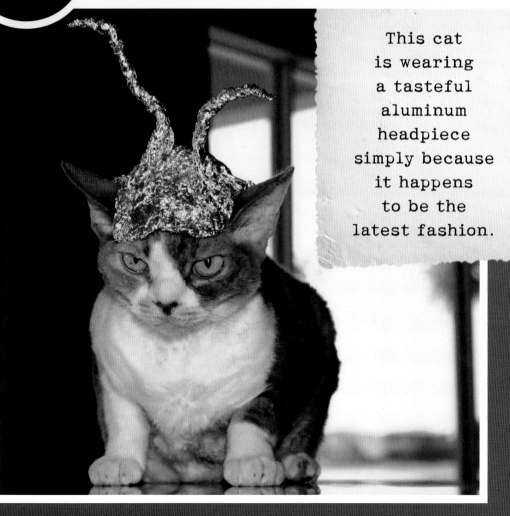

On the other hand, this poor, deluded animal believes her tinfoil hat will protect her from aliens and government conspiracies.

Chapter SEVEN

ADAPTABILITY

When the situation calls for it, cats are extremely capable of blending seamlessly into their surroundings, diplomatically adapting themselves to a social situation, or camouflaging themselves to fit into their physical surroundings. This can be very nice if you happen to have guests over for dinner.

Dogs, on the other hand, can be counted on to guffaw when the situation calls for gravity, to stick out when the situation calls for stealth, and to chase after squirrels when the situation calls for not chasing after squirrels. And when you have important guests over for dinner, dogs are as likely as not to attempt to lick their faces.

REASON #46

Cats are incredible at camouflage.

For this photo, which was supposed to be part of
a series on dogs' pathetic attempts at camouflage,
the dog didn't even bother to show up.

Cats are so attuned
to their
environment
that they can blend
in almost to
the point
of invisibility.

Cats know how to dress for the occasion.

Here, an office worker and his human colleague pose appropriately for a company photo.

This dog thought it was acceptable to show up at the office completely naked except for a collar.

REASON #48

Cats are masters of disguise.

You could be forgiven
for thinking that this is just a picture
of a sink full of dishes,
but it is actually a picture of a cat
disguised as a sink full of dishes.

This dog, disguised as your date for tonight,
is fooling no one.

  The ultimate masters of disguise are ocicats. While they appear to be wild, they actually don't possess any wild DNA.

Cats are incredible with costumes.

Despite a natural disinclination to dress up, this cat was able to transform himself for Halloween into the very likeness of a majestic lion roaming the savanna.

Dogs should never
be allowed to dress up.

REASON #50

Cats blend in.

No matter the situation, cats will always find a way to blend in so artfully that most people will assume they are a part of the surroundings.

Dogs don't even have the decency to be there
when you are trying to photograph them.

REASON #51

Cats can effectively hide themselves in any surroundings.

To an untrained eye, the photo below may appear to merely show a dog on a couch making a desperate plea for attention. If you look very, very carefully, however, there is also a cat hidden from view—like a ninja— waiting for her moment.

Canine attempts at hiding are
almost invariably spoiled
by embarrassing oversights.

REASON #52

Cats are patient hunters.

Just as in the wild,
domestic cats are capable of stalking
a slice of pizza or a sandwich
for hours at a time.

In a similar fashion, dogs are not completely inept at hunting for food, but they have no subtlety.

 The reason your cat is such an excellent pizza hunter is because he has 200 million scent cells on his nose. (For reference, you have just 5 million.)

Chapter EIGHT

WORK ETHIC

It's true that cats can often be seen sitting on the bed for days at a time, but this isn't because they are lazy—it's because they're *ideating*. They're taking a step back and thinking outside the box. They're leveraging their brain space to generate idea flow from the top level. It's all extremely complicated, but the point is that it requires a comfortable sofa and a lot of uninterrupted time to do properly.

A dog's idea of "hard work" is as laughable as a cat's is laudable. For most dogs, a day at the office is a roaring success if they've managed to intimidate a squirrel. This is why you never find dogs in management positions.

REASON #53

Cats are extremely hard workers.

This cat is so exhausted from a grueling day in the cat mines that she was unable even to reach her bed before passing out for a few short hours of rest.

Meanwhile, this stay-at-home dog was too lazy to move,
even as the bed was made around him.

Fat cats snooze more than skinny cats. Sounds about right.

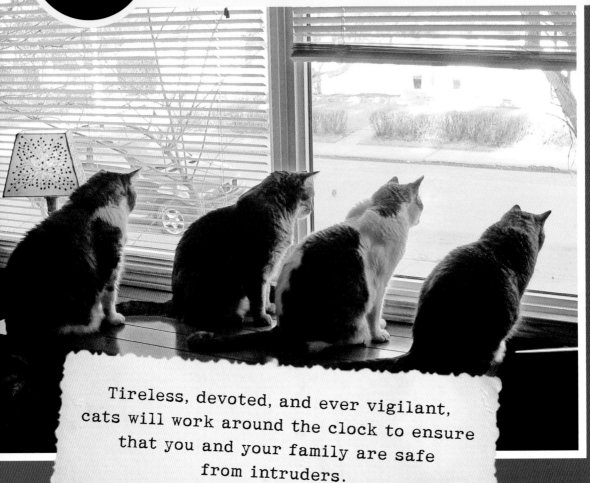

REASON #54

Cats will keep watch through the night.

Tireless, devoted, and ever vigilant, cats will work around the clock to ensure that you and your family are safe from intruders.

Dogs? Not so much.

REASON #55

Cats make amazing colleagues.

This office assistant cat stayed up all night to ensure that the monthly sales report is going to be a big hit with the board of directors.

This office assistant dog
stayed up all night drinking.

REASON #56

Cats keep long hours at the office.

Here, a young cat puts the finishing touches on a monthly report that will save her company from bankruptcy while her human colleague slowly falls asleep.

This dog's computer isn't even plugged in.

REASON #57

Dogs are terrible in meetings.

Dogs are renowned for scheduling meetings
just for the hell of it and then
showing up with no agenda.

Whereas if you're lucky enough to have a cat for a colleague, you will come to regard the regular brainstorming sessions they run as the highlight of your week.

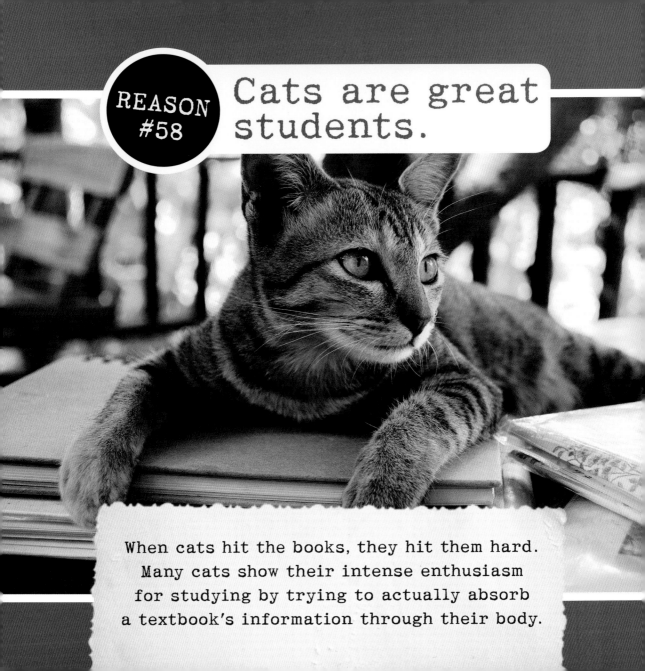

REASON #58

Cats are great students.

When cats hit the books, they hit them hard.
Many cats show their intense enthusiasm
for studying by trying to actually absorb
a textbook's information through their body.

Dogs don't really believe
in "book learning,"
but they can recite
Simpsons episodes from memory.

REASON #59

Cats will help you screen your calls.

As secretaries, cats have many fine qualities,
but perhaps the most impressive
is their ability to diligently and effectively
screen your calls so you never have to
deal with annoying interruptions.

If you let a dog anywhere near your phone,
he will use it to call expensive
and embarrassing 1-900 numbers.

PARENTING

Unlike dogs, who are allowed to run wild and given basically no guidance at all, every kitten is taught, from a very early age, the three principles that make great cats: 1) The best way to get someone to pay attention to you is to ignore them. 2) Sleeping is underrated. And 3) When in doubt, wash yourself. Can you imagine what a paradise society would be if we humans taught our children these principles with the same diligence that cats do? Everyone would be clean and well rested, and no one would bother anyone. Doesn't that sound nice?

REASON #60

Cats are concerned about education.

Here, a doting father cat teaches his child how to look worriedly out across the lawn at squirrels—an essential part of any kitten's journey as she learns how to cat.

This dog is trying to teach
a baby to do his bidding.

REASON #61

Cats make time to have dinner with their families.

This touching photo shows a loving cat mom sitting down at the head of the table as she waits for her children to join her.

Most dog children eat off
the *floor* while their parents
watch television.

REASON #62

A cat's parenting instinct kicks in regardless of species.

This picture shows a loving cat who has raised an abandoned human child in the wild as her own. As a result, the child will have more opportunities for success in life and business than if she had been raised by her natural parents.

Here, a dog teaches some human children
how to make a mess.

A mama cat is called a queen or a dam. Dad is called a tom or a sire. Cats are pretty fancy with their titles.

REASON #63

Dog children can't be left alone, even for a second.

These well-raised cat children (or "kittens") have used their alone time to creatively redecorate the bathroom.

As a direct result of bad parenting, this dog child (or "dogspawn") commits senseless acts of vandalism the moment she is left alone.

REASON #64

Cats are fiercely protective parents.

Mother cats love their kittens
almost as much as they love giving
penetrating death stares to anyone
with the temerity to mess with them.

This mother dog is enjoying
a delicious margarita while her puppies
talk to strangers.

REASON #65

Cat parents throw the best birthday parties.

Scenes from cat birthdays are heartwarming memories that will be cherished by cat parents and cat children alike for years to come.

These dog adolescents, known as "The Birthday Gang," make a mockery of a beautiful tradition by terrorizing the neighborhood in their signature gang hats.

Cats really do care! Science is not quite sure why, but cats like to

REASON #66

Cats ensure their children have ample time to play.

In this photo, a kitten enjoys herself in a play area that her parents have built and laboriously tested for safety.

This pug puppy has been deposited
in a "swing cage" while his parents watch a movie.

REASON #67

Cats have endless supplies of love.

No matter how hard it is or how much work it takes, cats will do everything to provide for their children because they love them unconditionally.

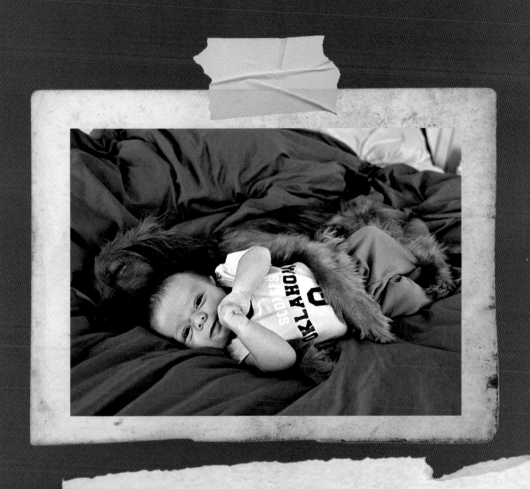

Without the slightest hesitation,
dogs will often abandon their own children
for the first interesting looking human baby
they come across, as this reprehensible
photo demonstrates.

Jack Shepherd is the Editorial Director at BuzzFeed. Shepherd joined BuzzFeed in 2008 and launched the site's Animals section in 2012. He lives in Brooklyn, with his cats and his regrets.

illustrations credits

67 REASONS WHY CATS ARE BETTER THAN DOGS
JACK SHEPHERD

Published by the National Geographic Society
1145 17th Street N.W., Washington, D.C. 20036

ISBN: 978-1-4262-1386-1

The National Geographic Society is one of the world's largest nonprofit scientific and educational organizations. Its mission is to inspire people to care about the planet. Founded in 1888, the Society is member supported and offers a community for members to get closer to explorers, connect with other members, and help make a difference. The Society reaches more than 450 million people worldwide each month through *National Geographic* and other magazines; National Geographic Channel; television documentaries; music; radio; films; books; DVDs; maps; exhibitions; live events; school publishing programs; interactive media; and merchandise. National Geographic has funded more than 10,000 scientific research, conservation, and exploration projects and supports an education program promoting geographic literacy. For more information, visit www.nationalgeographic.com.

National Geographic Society
1145 17th Street N.W.
Washington, D.C. 20036-4688 U.S.A.

For information about special discounts for bulk purchases, please contact National Geographic Books Special Sales: ngspecsales@ngs.org

For rights or permissions inquiries, please contact National Geographic Books Subsidiary Rights: ngbookrights@ngs.org

Interior design: Sanáa Akkach

Printed in Hong Kong

14/THK/1